ONE MOTIVATIONAL TIP FOR EACH DAY OF THE YEAR!

365 TIPS

TO HELP YOU MEMORISE THE QUR'AN

IS'HAAQ JASAT

First Published in Great Britain
by National Huffadh Association UK, 2020
www.ukhuffadh.org

Printing by The Olive Studio

Design & Typesetting by El Badr Institute UK
info@elbadr.co.uk

Proofreading & Editing by Wordsmiths Editing LTD

Referencing by Shaykh Khalil ibn Elyas Laher

All Rights Reserved

No part of this publication may be reproduced, stored or introduced
into a retrieval system, or transmitted, in any form or by any means,
without the prior written permission of both the copyright owner
and the publisher of this book.

Copyright © Is'Haaq Jasat

ISBN 978-1-5272-6053-5

For all sales and wholesale enquiries, please contact:
info@ukhuffadh.org
+447957734732

Follow this book on Instagram:
@hifdhtips365

CONTENTS

FOREWORD

Alhumdulillah, having read the book by my honourable and respected colleague Qari Is'Haaq Jasat, I can say that the book is an excellent and apt guide for parents and children. Qari Is'Haaq has put together an encyclopedia of words of wisdom and advice and great guidance for all those embarking on the journey to memorise the Holy Qur'an.

Today, there is a great demand and urgency of every parent wanting their child to be a Hafidh of the Qur'an. Qari Is'Haaq articulately and eloquently depicts the path to fulfil this desire. Many people boast of having a degree or certificate from top-class universities, such as Oxford and Harvard. One who memorises the Qur'an actually has a Sanad (chain of narration) which links back to the Companions (Allah be pleased with them) and to the Prophet (peace and blessings be upon him). One should reflect on this beautiful connection and strive for it personally.

I strongly recommend utilising this book as an instrumental tool to aid you in hifdh, there are also other books and gadgets to help you memorise. Even if you are not memorising the whole Qur'an, just a few Surahs or Juz 'Amma, this book can still be utilised. For those parents or children who have not thought about Hifdh or do not currently have a hafidh/hafidhah in the family, I urge you to consider it for your son or daughter as long as they are capable. Every family should endeavour to have one hafidh/hafidhah.

Finally, as a reminder to myself first and foremost, let us keep the intention for Hifdh, the pleasure of Allah SWT.

(Mufti) Ismail ibn Nazir Satia, Blackburn (United Kingdom)
(one who is in dire need of Allah's forgiveness, mercy and pleasure)

Author of 'I want My Child To Be A Hafidh'

PRAISE FOR 365 TIPS BY IS'HAAQ JASAT

This book provides anecdotes which grip the imagination of the user. It motivates and stimulates the mind. It reads as though a friend is always present supporting the reader in the learning of the Holy Qur'an. It is clear that thought and consideration has been entwined into the prose to make the book as approachable as possible, and suitable for all stages in the memorisation of Qur'an."

- MERAJUR CHOWDHURY, Director - Al Isharah Deaf Charity

It is a great and simple book full of tips extremely suitable for young huffadh. As a mother, I would definitely share it with my son who is thirteen and on his hifdz journey. As a Quran teacher, I would surely share it with my teen students! Thank you for sharing the book with me. May Allah bless this effort."

HAJAH NUR ZAHIRAH BINTI M SUKRAN , Co-founder & CEO
iluvQuran Tahfiz Centre, Malaysia

Qari Is'Haaq has devoted his time to the Qur'an and the humble efforts of National Huffadh Association UK. Years of experience now culminating in this wonderful collection of thoughts and insight that will help motivate and inspire those who are on their journey of memorising the Quran. We ask you to keep supporting our cause to protect, preserve and promote the Holy Qur'an and keep us in your duaas, wherever you are."

Board of Directors - National Huffadh Association UK

Fundamentals are the key to success. This book will inspire many."

- (QARI) ILYAAS EL BADR, Director - El Badr Institute

Alhamdulillah this book is an amazing guide for anybody who is thinking of starting their hifdh journey, or for the ones already on this blessed journey. InshaAllah this book will serve as motivation and encouragement for those who wish to fulfill this blessed task of memorising the beautiful book of Allah."

MOHSIN, Founder - Quran Cube

Alhamdulillah I have been waiting for someone to produce such a book that not only inspires those who just started to memorise the Qur'an or thinking about doing so but for those who are on this long journey, I only wish I had discovered such a book before my son had started memorising the Qur'an, as it would have been a fantastic guide for him."

- ABU YOUNUS, Father of Hafiz Mohammad Younus Rahman

A must read for a source of inspiration, dip into whenever you need some motivation to keep you going with your memorisation and revision of the Quran."

- (SHAYKH) KHALIL IBN ELYAS LAHER

"May Allah SWT make the 365 Tips To Help You Memorise The Qur'an book useful and beneficial InshaAllah for all. May He accept and allow many people to benefit from this book."

- DR MUFTI ABDUR RAHMAN IBN YUSUF MANGERA (U
Founder - Zamzamacademy.com & Whitethread Institu

"May Allah bless the author for all the good work he has done. I am a Hifdh student and will definitely be reading this book daily for motivation."

- IKRAM HSINI, Belgiu

"This is a first of a kind book I have seen that truly acts like a guide for you in your jour ney to memorizing the Qur'an Al Kareem. 365 Tips not only holds your finger, but fills that void that you have some inspiration everyday, not once a week, but everyday."

- HAFIDH WASIF KHAN, CEO - Mashaer Travel, U

"Congratulations on this new book. Allah put barakah in it and accept it. Allah make it reach all the huffaz far and wide and make it an essential tool for their success."

- MUHAMMAD QASIM, Teacher - An Nasihah Leicester (U

"His love for the ummah is his motivation in producing such a master piece 365 Tips. T book gives valuable and encouraging tips for every day of the year; hence its title. Is'Haaq's own journey the successes and pitfalls is what shapes this book and allows hi to guide Hifzs students because he is aware of how easy it is to become frustrated. The daily tips will certainly help."

- BIBI RABBIYAH KHAN, President - Wightman Road Mosq
London Islamic Cultural Soci

ACKNOWLEDGEMENTS

"Whoever does not thank people has not thanked Allah." – Prophet Muhammad PBUH (Sunan Abi Dawud)

Alhamdulillah I am very grateful to The Almighty for allowing me to write this book, which is the final product of a very challenging but rewarding journey. However, it would not be befitting if I did not mention specific individuals who have inspired and supported me in the writing of this book.

Therefore, I am very grateful and feel a deep sense of gratitude to the following individuals:

-to my beloved wife Aishahbibi and our daughter Rahmiyyah for sacrificing the time that I spent in writing and compiling this book. They have both been huge pillars of support.

-to my esteemed and honourable teacher Mawlana Qari Ilyas Adam Gati (who was my hifdh teacher) for his endless and unconditional love, patience, support, motivation and encouragement. I am indebted to him always. May Allah grant him a healthy and long life.

-to Quwwat ul Islam Mosque in London for allowing me to study within the Madrasah and to memorise the Qur'an. In particular, I would like to thank my beloved teachers: Shaykh ul Hadeeth Mawlana Saleem Nawab, Mawlana Abdul Mateen Bhuta and Mawlana Yunus Dudhwala.

-to my late grandfather Mawlana Qari Fateh Mohammad Laher (may Allah have mercy on him) for inspiring me with his wisdom, intellect and knowledge. He made lots of du'as for me and my siblings when we were younger to continue the work of the deen.

-to my mother for her continuous sacrifices in waking me up every morning so that I can attend my daily hifdh class and to my father for his constant support and prayers.

-to my mother in-law and my late father in-law for their constant support, encouragement and words of wisdom.

-to my brothers, sisters and all immediate/extended family members for always believing in my work and encouraging me to progress.

-to my brothers and dear colleagues from the National Huffadh Association UK; Jamal, Moossa and Sultan, who have always supported and lent their advice whenever needed for this project.

-to my beloved cousin for playing an instrumental part since the inception of National Huffadh Association UK and for always overlooking and maintaining our website, printing and design work.

-to my dear brother Qari Ilyaas El Badr for being the driving force behind the design and branding element of this book, as well as for the National Huffadh Association UK.

-to my dear brother Salah Sharief and the Wordsmiths team for their attention to detail in terms of the proofreading and editing of this book.

-to beloved Dr Mufti Abdur Rahman ibn Yusuf for his constant support, guidance and du'as since the inception of National Huffadh Association UK.

-to my dear brother Zain Luqman Miah and his Launchgood team for helping me to facilitate a global reach for this book.

- to the additional group of proofreaders who gave valuable feedback to me throughout the composition of this book: Abu Younus, Ustadah Nur Zahirah M Sukran, Shaykh Khalid ibn Elyas Laher, Mufti Ismail ibn Nazir Satia, Jamal Mannan, Meraj Chowdhury, Shabnam Aslam and Mawlana Yahya Nadat.

-to all the supporters and members of the National Huffadh Association UK for continuously following and sharing our work around the UK and the rest of the world.

INTRODUCTION

Millions of Muslims from around the world have memorised the Qur'an. This is by no means an easy feat and not every person is blessed with the gift of being a Hafidh or a Hafidhah. It takes a lot of dedication, motivation and hard work.

From the time of our beloved Prophet Muhammad PBUH (over 1400 years ago) up until now, times have changed. Technology and learning methods have evolved. Nowadays, there are many advanced methods of undertaking a Hifdh program. There are more support methods and networks available for students who wish to memorise the Qur'an.

Alhamdulillah, I completed my Hifdh journey and memorized the entire Qur'an at a young age of 12.However, especially in my days of learning (around the year 2001), there were very limited resources available for Hifdh students. Nowadays, we have so much information and resources at the click of a button, right at our fingertips. Technology has advanced rapidly over the years as well.

The aim of this book is to support and motivate anyone who wishes to either memorise or retain their memory of the Qur'an. Whether you are a Hifdh student or have already become a Hafidh/Hafidhah, this book will InshaAllah guide and support you in your Hifdh journey.

The concept of 365 tips is quite simple; one inspirational tip for every day of the year. There may be days when you feel frustrated or feel like giving up in your Hifdh journey. However, these daily tips will hopefully give you a sense of motivation and dedication in developing yourself as a Hifdh student. Also, for those who have memorised the Qur'an, you will always remain a student of the Qur'an and there will be enough Qur'anic knowledge, even after you complete your Hifdh.

I want to share a very beautiful and inspirational piece of advice which my Ustadh (May Allah always bless him and grant him a long life) mentioned to us once during our time of undertaking the Hifdh studies: "This is the easiest part, memorising the Qur'an. The hardest part is when you complete memorising the entire Qur'an. Because then it becomes your lifelong responsibility to retain every single letter that you have memorised until the day you depart from this world." The Qur'an is not to be mastered, rather it masters you.

Please kindly forgive me for any shortcomings and mistakes made in this book.

A humble request for duaas.

Is'Haaq Jasat (Founder CEO, National Huffadh Association UK)

28 Jumada Al Akhirah 1441
Sunday 23rd February 2020

PREPARATION AND INTENTION

This section aims to equip you with a strong foundation for when you commence your Qur'an memorisation journey. Many people are often puzzled and unsure of how to start memorising the Qur'an. Many questions go through one's mind: How? Why? Where? When?

Well, the key to ensuring a successful journey is by preparing in the best way possible. You must undertake as much research as possible, prior to starting the memorisation journey. Naturally, you will have doubts and negative thoughts. But try to think positively and remind yourself as to why you are undertaking this beautiful journey, it is ultimately to please The Almighty.

Preparing also involves adjusting your daily routine, spending more time with the Qur'an and maybe even trying to memorise some sections of the Qur'an prior to commencing your hifdh journey. Such practices will definitely prepare you more and provide you with even more confidence. Supplicating to Allah daily is also a form of preparation. Ask Him to help you prepare as much as possible.

Your intention is the most important part of the Qur'an memorisation journey. It needs to be pure, sincere and true. Intend to change yourself for the better and build an intellectual understanding of the journey, as this journey could potentially change your entire life forever. Be firm in your intention and keep it as pure as possible. Good deeds with sincere intentions are most likely to be rewarded by Allah even more.

 # WEEK ONE

TIP 1:
"Always practice with a pure heart and sincere intention that you are undertaking the hifdh journey for the sake of Allah alone. There is no other objective or reward sought apart from Allah's ultimate reward."

TIP 2:
"Do not start your hifdh journey just because your parents or friends have done so. You are your own person. Do it because YOU wish to do so!"

TIP 3:
"Being mentally focused is essential. Clear your mind of any doubts and negative thoughts. Having a clean mind will help you to engage in a productive hifdh journey."

TIP 4:
"Seeking advice from reliable family members and friends before undertaking the hifdh journey is very helpful. Ask them to highlight your strengths and weaknesses."

TIP 5:
"A good way to prepare for your hifdh journey is to extensively read and research the history and facts of the Qur'an. Get to know this book more and develop your knowledge further."

TIP 6:
"An effective preparation technique is to maintain a consistent daily recitation of the Qur'an. This will increase your familiarity with the words of the Qur'an."

TIP 7:
"You are never too young or too old to start preparing for your hifdh journey. Allah blesses each person differently with regards their memory. Age is nothing but a number!"

 # WEEK TWO

TIP 8:
"Always check and renew your intention during your hifdh journey. Did you undertake this journey for fame or status? If it was not for Allah then will the Qur'an intercede for or against you on the Day of Reckoning?"

TIP 9:
"Prepare yourself spiritually prior to starting your hifdh journey. Try to become closer to Allah than before. Grow and develop your spiritual state."

TIP 10:
"Preparing yourself physically is essential. Assess your current diet and eating routine. Eating foods known to improve memory will help you in the long term."

TIP 11:
"Prior to undertaking the hifdh journey, ask yourself how long will it take you to complete your Qur'an memorisation? Take a calculated guess and use this as a starting point."

TIP 12:
"You have to prepare daily du'as to Allah prior to starting your hifdh journey. Ask Allah to help and guide you every step of the way."

TIP 13:
"It is always good practice to memorise some Surahs of the Qur'an before commencing the hifdh journey. This will ensure you are adequately prepared and motivate you to continue!"

TIP 14:
"Listening to music regularly affects the retention of Qur'an in one's mind. Think hard about sacrificing this bad habit prior to commencing the hifdh journey."

TIP 15:
"Before commencing your hifdh journey, you will need to sacrifice time every day to prepare for what is to come. It will not be easy but time management is key."

TIP 16:
"Do not rush into starting your hifdh journey. Give yourself sufficient time to plan and prepare how you will embark on the process."

TIP 17:
"One good way to prepare is to visit other hifdh institutions to gain a feel of the environment and learning systems involved. It will also motivate you further!"

TIP 18:
"Commit to your hifdh journey mentally. Continuously remind yourself why you wish to pursue this noble deed. Always remain focused."

TIP 19:
"Research the various learning methods available for Qur'an memorisation. Is there a specific method which may work best for you? Try it!"

TIP 20:
"Being disciplined and ensuring you have ample rest is essential for a successful hifdh journey. Do you need to dedicate more sleeping hours from now?"

TIP 21:
"A useful preparation method is to use the same Qur'an throughout your hifdh journey. This will help you to remain consistent in your learning."

# WEEK FOUR

TIP 22:
"Before commencing your hifdh journey, ask for your parents' du'as. If they have passed away, continue to remember them each time you read the Qur'an."

TIP 23:
"The Qur'an will change your life remarkably. Have you changed parts of your life to reflect your hifdh journey? Strive to always be a person of the Qur'an."

TIP 24:
"If you are failing to plan, then you are planning to fail. So prepare and plan before you undertake your hifdh journey!"

TIP 25:
"Even if you are just thinking of memorising the Qur'an, Allah has blessed you. Remember, He only selects whomsoever He wishes to become a hafidh/hafidhah."

TIP 26:
"If you ever feel that your memory may be too weak to memorise the Qur'an, just remember that the Prophet Muhammad (PBUH) was illiterate and he was a hafidh!"

TIP 27:
"Do not expect to have the strongest memory immediately. Preparing a sharp memory takes a lot of time and effort. Keep at it daily and never give up!"

TIP 28:
"Having the correct intention, is the foundation of this journey. Keep on trying daily and leave the rest to Allah. He always assists those with sincere hearts."

# WEEK FIVE

TIP 29:
"At times, Shaitaan will try and make you think twice about preparing for your hifdh journey. As long as you have Allah and sincerity, you will overcome the Satanic whispers, inshaAllah!"

TIP 30:
"Ensure that your intention is not dominated by status, fame or materialistic aims. If you chase the world over the Qur'an, then you will not be attaining maximum rewards from Allah."

TIP 31:
"Starting your hifdh journey can be very daunting and challenging. Make the right intention and take the first step towards memorising the Qur'an. Allah's Help is never far away!"

TIP 32:
"The hifdh journey is for you. Not to please others. It will benefit you spiritually in this world and the next. Keep the intention solely between you and Allah, nobody else."

TIP 33:
"Preparing for your hifdh journey is not going to be easy. You have never attempted this before, but with a sincere intention you will learn, develop and grow."

TIP 34:
"Do not let your past overcome your desire to start memorising the Qur'an. If Allah can guide the likes of Umar (RA), how can He not guide you through the Qur'an?"

TIP 35:
"There is a big difference between an intention and actually carrying out the practical element of the intention. Ask Allah to grant you the reality of the intention daily."

# WEEK SIX

TIP 36:
"Some friends or family members may mock and discourage you from undertaking the hifdh journey. Do not get diverted and turn to Allah for strength. Keep on going!"

TIP 37:
"When preparing for the hifdh journey, keep on reminding yourself that your entire life will change for the better. The Qur'an must be the focal point of your life!"

TIP 38:
"When you memorise the first verse of the Qur'an, you may look and take account of all the thousands of verses remaining that you are yet to memorise. Approach each verse one at a time. You will get there soon, inshaAllah."

TIP 39:
"The early preparation stages require the most patience and dedication. This will ultimately set a solid foundation for the remaining hifdh journey."

TIP 40:
"Prepare with the utmost confidence. Believe that you can memorise the Qur'an. Always keep yourself motivated. Continue looking forward and never look back."

TIP 41:
Abdullah ibn Mas'ud said:
"When a man amongst us learnt ten verses from the Qur'an, he would not move on to the next verses until he had understood their meanings and how to act by them."
(Al Tabari, Al Tafsir 1:80)

TIP 42:
Prophet Muhammad (PBUH) said:
"The best amongst you is he who learns the Qur'an and teaches it."
(Bukhari, Abu Dawud & Tirmidhi)

INSPIRATIONAL ADVICE FROM THE PAST

One of the inspirational aspects of Islam is the beauty and richness in our history. We are so fortunate to have had such motivational and courageous individuals who have contributed so positively to the progress of Islam throughout the world.

This section seeks to provide sources of inspiration and motivation through the advice of our predecessors. There is so much to learn and bring into our lives. Every piece of advice and tip shared within this section is connected to the Qur'an memorisation journey. InshaAllah this advice will assist you greatly in your journey.

Ultimately, we would not be Muslims today if it was not for the struggles and challenges our beloved Prophet Muhammad (PBUH) and his companions encountered throughout their lives. Their sacrifices are remembered today and we should always appreciate and value their contributions to Islam.

In particular regarding how the Qur'an was compiled, one cannot doubt the true love and value our predecessors had for this beautiful book. In fact, it was our beloved Prophet Muhammad (PBUH) who mentioned within his final sermon that: 'If you hold onto the Qur'an and Sunnah, you will never go astray.'

In reality, it is our lifelong duty to protect and preserve the Qur'an.

WEEK SEVEN

TIP 43:
Abdullah ibn Mas'ud said: "A memoriser of the Qur'an should be known for his long night prayers when people are asleep. His fasting when people are eating, his sadness when people are happy, his silence when people are talking nonsense, and his humbleness when people are not. He should be wise, gentle, and not talk too much: he should not be rude, negligent, clamorous, nor hot tempered."
(Ibn al Jawzee, Sifaat as-Safwa: 1/413)

TIP 44:
Prophet Muhammad (PBUH) said: "The one who is proficient in the recitation of the Qur'an will be with the honourable and obedient scribes (angels) and he who recites the Qur'an and finds it difficult to recite, he will have a double reward."
(Al Bukhari & Muslim)

TIP 45:
"Do not scatter the Qur'an like inferior dates and do not chant it as quickly as with poetry. Stop and marvel at its wonders, move hearts with it and do not let your concern be the end of the Surah."
(Abdullah ibn Mas'ud (RA))

TIP 46:
"The memoriser of the Qur'an carries the flag of Islam. He shouldn't waste his time in vain amusement, distractions and pointless matters with those who do so, out of respect for the Qur'an."
(Al Fudhayl bin 'Iyaad)

TIP 47:
"Do not be fooled by the one who recites the Qur'an. His recitation is but speech. But rather, look to those who act according to it."
(Umar ibn Khattab (RA))

TIP 48:
"And we have made the Qur'an easy for remembrance, so is there anyone who will remember?"
(Qur'an 54:17)

TIP 49:
"Abdullah ibn 'Amr said that the Prophet (peace and blessings of Allah be upon him) said: "It will be said to the companion of the Qur'an (i.e., the one who memorised and studied it): 'Read, advance in status and recite as you used to do in the world, for your status will be commensurate with the last aayah that you recite."
(Narrated by al-Tirmidhi)

WEEK EIGHT

TIP 50:
"Knowledge is not measured by how much is memorised, but rather by how much it is acted on." (Imam Shafi'ee)

TIP 51:
"Without knowledge, action is useless and knowledge without action is futile." (Abu Bakr (RA))

TIP 52:
"Knowledge is that which benefits, not that which is memorised." (Imam Shafi'ee)

TIP 53:
"When Aishah (RA) was asked about the character of the Prophet Muhammad (PBUH), she replied 'The Qur'an'.

TIP 54:
"I leave behind with me two things; the Qur'an and Sunnah. If you follow these, you will never go astray." (Prophet Muhammad (PBUH))

TIP 55:
"Allah does not burden a soul more than it can bear." (Qur'an – 2: 286)

TIP 56:
"And ease for me my task" (Taha – 20:26)

 # WEEK NINE

TIP 57:
"Do what is beautiful. Allah loves those who do what is beautiful." (Qur'an – 2:195)

TIP 58:
"And My Mercy encompasses everything." (Qur'an – 7:156)

TIP 59:
"So, verily with hardship there is relief. Verily, with hardship there is relief." (Qur'an – 94:5-6)

TIP 60:
"Or a little more, and recite the Qur'an aloud in a slow, pleasant tone and style." (Qur'an – 73:4)

TIP 61:
"The people of the Qur'an are those who read it and act upon it, even if they haven't memorised it." (Ibn Al Qayyim (RA))

TIP 62:
"Whoever reads the Qur'an and memorises it, Allah will admit him into Paradise and allow him to intercede for ten of his family members who all deserved to enter Hell." (Ibn Majah)

TIP 63:
"The most excellent of you is the one who learns the Qur'an and teaches it." (Prophet Muhammad (PBUH))

 # WEEK TEN

TIP 64:
"And We send down from the Qur'an that which is a healing and a mercy to those who believe....." (17:82)

TIP 65:
"Suwayd ibn 'Abd al-'Azeez said: When Abu'd-Darda' had prayed Fajr in the mosque of Damascus, the people would gather to learn Qur'an from him, so he would put them into groups of ten, with an instructor for each group, and he would stand in the mihrab watching them. If one of them made a mistake, he would refer to his instructor, and if the instructor made a mistake, he would refer to Abu'd-Darda' and ask him about that."

TIP 66:
"It was narrated that Ibn Mashkam said: Abu'd-Darda' said to me: Count those who are studying the Qur'an with me. I counted them, and they were over one thousand and six hundred, and for each group of ten there was a teacher." (Marifat al-Qurra al-Kibaar)

TIP 67:
"Abu 'Abd ar-Rahmaan as-Sulami said: Those who used to teach us the Qur'an (including reciting and memorising) told us that they used to learn it from the Prophet (PBUH). When they learned ten verses, they would not move on until they put into practice what those verses said, so we used to learn the Qur'an and how to act upon its teachings together."

TIP 68:
"One who often thinks and reflects, develops his foresight and vision." (Hazrat Ali (RA))

TIP 69:
"The most beloved deeds to Allah are those done regularly, no matter how small." (Bukhari & Muslim)

TIP 70:
"There is no better beauty than intellect." (Prophet Muhammad (PBUH))

 # WEEK ELEVEN

TIP 71:
"Sometimes people with the worst past can create the best future." (Umar ibn Khattab (RA))

TIP 72:
"Verily, this is a Book in which there is no doubt." (2:2)

TIP 73:
"Recite the Qur'an, for it will intercede for you on the Day of Judgement." (Muslim)

TIP 74:
"So when the Qur'an is being recited, then listen to it and pay attention that you may receive mercy." (Qur'an 7:204)

TIP 75:
"The Prophet Muhammad (PBUH) said; "Whoever recites a letter from the book of Allah, he will be credited with a good deed and a good deed gets a ten-fold reward. I do not say Alif-Laam-Meem is one letter but Alif is a letter, Laam is a letter and Meem is a letter."

TIP 76:
"The Prophet Muhammad (PBUH) said: "Everything has a heart and the heart of the Glorious Qur'an is Surah Yaseen. Whoever reads Surah Yaseen, Allah records for them a reward equal to that of reading the whole Qur'an 10 times." (Tirmidhi)

TIP 77:
"It will be said to the companion of the Qur'an: Recite and rise in status, recite as you used to recite in the world, for your status will be the last verse that you recite."

CHOOSING THE RIGHT SCHOOL AND TEACHER

Each learner is different. We all have our own learning methods and needs. Therefore, it is imperative that you only select a teacher based on your style of learning. Ultimately, it is you as a student who will be progressing and learning daily at the feet of your teacher. The golden rule is to ensure that no matter which teacher you choose for your Qur'an memorisation journey, you must always honour and respect your beloved teacher.

One of the key reasons for including this section is that there are many students who struggle to progress or focus in the classroom because their relationship and connection with the teacher is not evident. Moreover, the school environment may not be suited to their needs. It is also vital that the mutual respect between a student and a teacher is always present.

Some students find it more productive to learn at home in a space which they feel much more comfortable in, while other students may prefer a smaller class size. Do not be shy about selecting the school you deem the most suitable for you. Following your friends or family members' footsteps is not always the wisest choice. Select the school which is right for your learning.

You should always be humble in front of your teacher. Never disrespect or display arrogance in front of your teacher. Remember, if your teacher is happy with you, then Allah is happy with you.

# WEEK TWELVE

TIP 78:
"There is only so much one can learn by reciting Qur'an him/herself. Enrolling into a hifdh school will help to facilitate the Qur'an memorisation journey."

TIP 79:
"Understanding the structure and systems of a hifdh school is essential. Undertake as much research as possible about the hifdh school before selecting which one to enrol in."

TIP 80:
"Do not hold back on any queries you may have. Clarify any misconceptions or queries prior to enrolling into a hifdh school.

TIP 81:
"Not every hifdh school is easy at the beginning. Therefore, do not be disheartened if you do not settle into a hifdh school immediately. Give it time and keep on trying."

TIP 82:
"Ease of distance can help you to save time and focus more on your hifdh journey. Try to find a hifdh school which is fairly close to your home."

TIP 83:
"Do not enrol into a hifdh school just because a friend or a family member has studied or is studying there. The intention needs to solely be for yourself and do not rely on anybody else."

TIP 84:
"Time management is essential. Being punctual daily to your hifdh school will set a strong foundation for your learning journey of memorising the Qur'an."

WEEK THIRTEEN

TIP 85:
"Respect and value the policies and procedures of the hifdh school. Being fully compliant will demonstrate core principles within yourself as a Qur'an student."

TIP 86:
"Embracing the learning culture of the hifdh school is important. Try to adapt to the various learning methods used by the hifdh school."

TIP 87:
"Your Qur'an memorisation journey is never going to just be easy. You will face hardships at your hifdh school. Be patient and learn to overcome these.

TIP 88:
"Remember, even when you are outside of the hifdh school, you are still representing your institution. Always act like a person of the Qur'an."

TIP 89:
"A good way to settle into a new hifdh school is by befriending elder and experienced hifdh students. Sit with them regularly and benefit from their knowledge and experience."

TIP 90:
"Try to establish an experienced mentor within your class. Someone who can help to develop your knowledge, learning and character."

TIP 91:
"Always be disciplined with your daily routines. Set yourself realistic targets for progress in hifdh. Review them regularly with your teacher and aim to progress further."

# WEEK FOURTEEN

TIP 92:
"The smaller the class size, the more attention you will receive as a student. The larger the class size, the less focus on you. Each student learns and adapts in different classroom settings."

TIP 93:
"One-to-one teaching and learning is not suitable for everyone. However, one advantage of this method is that it provides exclusive and uninterrupted attention to develop your hifdh."

TIP 94:
"You may have tried learning at a hifdh school for a while but you are not progressing. Don't be afraid to explore other options. It may be that another hifdh school would be better suited for you!"

TIP 95:
"As a hifdh student, always remember that in a hifdh school you are not just being taught about Qur'anic principles but you are also being equipped for the principles of life."

TIP 96:
"A truly dedicated and committed hifdh student will never be able to forget the words of wisdom and advice bestowed by his or her teacher. Such advice remains with you for the rest of your life."

TIP 97:
"First impressions are crucial. At the very first meeting, aim to win over your teacher and initiate a bond from the offset. A teacher can learn a lot about a student from the very first encounter."

TIP 98:
"Sincerity and humility will carry a lot of weight. Especially when it comes to maintaining an effective relationship with your teacher. Stay humble and always be sincere in your words."

WEEK FIFTEEN

TIP 99:
"Nowadays, a common barrier to learning and progress in hifdh is the generation gap and language barrier. However, this can be overcome through wisdom and resilience."

TIP 100:
"There is no such thing as the perfect teacher. Never put your teacher on a pedestal and always be aware that he/she is human and is prone to making mistakes, just like you."

TIP 101:
"Not everyone has the unique opportunity to be taught by just one hifdh teacher. Many students learn from several teachers throughout their hifdh studies. Everyone's journey is different."

TIP 102:
"Sometimes, it may take slightly longer to build an effective bond with your teacher. Do not force this to happen. When the time is right, The Almighty will permit your relationship to flourish."

TIP 103:
"At times, you may feel frustrated and upset by your teacher. Your mind may tell you to go through your hifdh journey alone. Stay strong and do not let the Satanic whispers get the better of you."

TIP 104:
"There is nothing wrong in confiding in your teacher for help and advice. Take that first step and confide, then see how your relationship will blossom and develop."

TIP 105:
"One of the key qualities of an effective teacher is understanding the strengths and weaknesses of each student. Thereafter, your teacher will inevitably tailor your learning based on your abilities."

WEEK SIXTEEN

TIP 106:
"The role of a hifdh teacher is not to memorise the Qur'an for you, but rather, to guide and nurture your learning and to help equip you with a strong memory and understanding of the Qur'an."

TIP 107:
"As a hifdh student, make it a daily habit to carefully observe and take heed of the advice given to other students. It could be that specific advice may help you in your hifdh journey specifically."

TIP 108:
"A teacher comes with years of experience. Value and cherish this. Appreciate the various types of students he or she has worked with over the years. Be patient and always work in cooperation."

TIP 109:
"One of the key responsibilities of a hifdh teacher is to try and ensure that you persist in your Qur'an memorisation right until the very end. Make the responsibility easier for him/her."

TIP 110:
"To become an effective hifdh teacher, essentially, you have to become a successful coach. Are you being coached? Does the input by your teacher reflect the progress you are making in class?"

TIP 111:
"The rapport between a teacher and a student is essential. As a student, you should never feel shy or reluctant to talk with your hifdh teacher. Always be comfortable and open about your feelings."

TIP 112:
"Never miss an opportunity to serve your teacher by doing khidmah. You never know, this very noble act could result in you attaining Paradise as a result. Allah knows best."

# WEEK SEVENTEEN

TIP 113:
"Another skill of an effective teacher is being able to intervene when a certain learning method is not progressing in the right direction. Work with your teacher and adapt to new learning strategies."

TIP 114:
"You have to gain the prayers of your teachers. This is so crucial for your hifdh journey. It may be that one prayer made by your teacher for you is accepted by Allah."

TIP 115:
"Attentiveness is the key to developing yourself in your hifdh journey. Be attentive to everything that your hifdh teacher does. There is a lesson to learn in every action."

TIP 116:
"Do not expect favouritism from your teacher. Expect your teacher to treat you exactly the same way as he or she would treat other students. Never think of yourself to be of a higher status than your peers."

TIP 117:
"Utilise the experience and skills of your teacher. Remember, one day you may be in your teacher's shoes and start a teaching career. Would you not want to embody your teacher's skills?"

TIP 118:
"As a hifdh student, aim to always excel and strive for excellence. If your teacher instructs you to learn one page of a new lesson, go that extra mile and learn some more. Always push yourself!"

TIP 119:
"Treat your teachers in exactly the same way that you treat your parents. Always respect their discipline, knowledge and status."

TAJWEED, REFLECTION AND CORRECT RECITATION

One of the most important aspects of a Qur'an memorisation journey is to also learn how to recite the Qur'an correctly. Moreover, understanding the words of the Qur'an is of even greater significance.

This section has been included to illustrate that the correct recitation of the Qur'an is a fundamental duty of every Muslim. Yes, there may be language barriers or you may not have had the appropriate guidance on how to recite the Qur'an correctly from a young age. But ultimately, it is your responsibility to learn how to recite the Qur'an in the way that was taught by our beloved Prophet Muhammad (PBUH). We cannot simply recite the Qur'an in any manner; reciting the Qur'an is also a form of respect.

Reflecting upon the Qur'an is essential. You can spend hours reciting the words of the Qur'an but if you have not truly understood what you are reciting, then how can you claim to truly love the Qur'an in its entirety? Imagine how close and deep your connection to Allah would be if you understood the words of the Qur'an.

WEEK EIGHTEEN

TIP 120:
"Always remember, you are reciting the very words of Allah. He is the One who is talking to us and He is the One who is protecting and preserving the Qur'an daily."

TIP 121:
"Everything in life has a certain code and a structure. You cannot simply recite the Qur'an in the manner that pleases you, rather you should recite the Qur'an in the manner taught by the Prophet (PBUH)."

TIP 122:
"Tajweed is the focal point of the Qur'an. To recite the Qur'an correctly, you must have a strong understanding of the tajweed rules. This is essential for any hifdh student."

TIP 123:
"For many hifdh students, tajweed may not be their strongest point. Many are taught the Qur'an in a certain manner which does not reflect the true regulations of tajweed. This must be overcome."

TIP 124:
"There is no such thing as the 'perfect tajweed." Possessing a strong understanding of tajweed requires a lot of commitment and dedication to learn and apply the rules into one's recitation."

TIP 125:
"As a hifdh student, daily practice in Qur'anic recitation is essential in developing one' application of tajweed rules. Recite, record and repeat. Try this daily."

TIP 126:
"One of the best methods to acquire a strong foundation of tajweed within your recitation is by listening frequently to renowned and qualified Qur'anic reciters, past or present."

WEEK NINETEEN

TIP 127:
"By reciting the Qur'an using the correct tajweed rules, you are demonstrating to Allah that you respect the Qur'an and the manner in which it was recited."

TIP 128:
"As a hifdh student, you need to be able to explain the various tajweed rules and how they apply respectively at their different places within the Qur'an. This is key."

TIP 129:
"Reciting the Qur'an correctly with tajweed requires a huge amount of discipline and understanding. Most importantly, you are reviving the manner in which the Qur'an was recited by the companions of the Prophet Muhammad (PBUH)."

TIP 130:
"If you are struggling to grasp the correct application of the relevant tajweed rules, it may be worth considering taking on additional lessons to help you to develop further."

TIP 131:
"Some hifdh institutions employ a 'tajweed coach'. Their job is to simply focus on improving and developing pupils' understanding and application of the correct tajweed rules. Does your hifdh school have one?

TIP 132:
"Reflecting upon the Qur'an is just as important as reciting the Qur'an correctly. Some would arguably say that reflection upon the words of the Qur'an is the most important duty."

TIP 133:
"Learning the Arabic language is crucial if you wish to understand and reflect upon the verses of the Qur'an. Every hifdh student should strive to gain a strong understanding of Arabic."

WEEK TWENTY

TIP 134:
"Imagine how fortunate the Arabs are. The vast majority of them are able to understand the words of the Qur'an. How would you feel if this beautiful book was revealed in your mother tongue?"

TIP 135:
"Reflecting upon the verses of the Qur'an should allow you to bring the qualities of the Qur'an into your life. How close or far away are you from implementing the Qur'an within your daily life?"

TIP 136:
"Remember, the companions of the Prophet Muhammad (PBUH) would often delay the memorisation of the next verse until they had implemented the meanings of the previous verses into their own lives."

TIP 137:
"It is never too late to learn the Arabic language. Allah says in the Qur'an that He has made the Qur'an easy for people to remember. Don't delay and start learning Arabic today!"

TIP 138:
"When you reflect upon the verses of the Qur'an, you will inevitably form a closer relationship with The Almighty and you will understand Him even better than before."

TIP 139:
"Reflecting and pondering over the Qur'anic verses displays a sense of inner development and growth. Try it and you will come to realise how your hifdh journey becomes even more meaningful."

TIP 140:
"One effective method used to enhance one's understanding of the Qur'an is by making a regular habit of reading the Qur'an in the language that you primarily speak in, as well as regularly reciting it in Arabic."

 # WEEK TWENTY ONE

TIP 141:
"The Qur'an can apply to any situation within our lives. Depending on how you are feeling or what you are going through, the Qur'an can be a source of comfort and guidance for you."

TIP 142:
"Imagine reading a book in a different language and find that you can read the words but you can't understand them. How will you be able to understand the words of the author? This is the same analogy with the Qur'an."

TIP 143:
"Develop a close relationship with the Qur'an through reflection and understanding. In return, see how your relationship with Allah develops."

TIP 144:
"There are many words of wisdom and precious messages contained within the Qur'an. If you truly reflect upon the Qur'an, you would understand these messages and fully take heed."

TIP 145:
"One good means of gaining a basic understanding of the Qur'an is by reading a Mushaf containing the Arabic language on one side and its translation in your language on the other."

TIP 146:
"When the companions of the Prophet Muhammad (PBUH) would recite the Qur'an, their faith would increase even more. Is this the case with your recitation?"

TIP 147:
"It is only by reflecting upon the verses of the Qur'an do we attain a closer connection with Allah. Should this not be our ultimate goal when undertaking our hifdh journey?"

TIP 148:
"Make the intention to start understanding the Qur'an at your own pace. Maybe one verse or one page a day to begin with and gradually build up a realistic routine."

TIP 149:
"One advantage of understanding and reflecting upon the verses of the Qur'an is that it will make your hifdh journey easier. You will understand the words as you memorise them."

TIP 150:
"You may initially find the Arabic language challenging and difficult to comprehend, but there is infinite wisdom behind Allah's plans. He has made the Qur'an easy for us to remember."

TIP 151:
"You may not speak Arabic as a first language, however, don't let that become a barrier to understanding the Qur'an more deeply. There are many who memorise the Qur'an easily and do not even speak a word of Arabic!"

TIP 152:
"Make a firm intention to recite the Qur'an daily with understanding. It will help to strengthen your faith and revolutionise your relationship with Allah."

TIP 153:
"Enrolling into a beginners' Arabic course will help you to develop a basic understanding of the key lessons from the Qur'an. Having another teacher will help you to gain more motivation too."

TIP 154:
"There is no better feeling than being able to recite the Qur'an proficiently with tajweed. However, ensure that you select a teacher who is qualified and proficient in the field of tajweed."

WEEK TWENTY THREE

TIP 155:
"Holding regular Qur'anic learning circles within the home can help to build your confidence and love for this beautiful book. Encourage and teach family members to recite the Qur'an correctly with understanding."

TIP 156:
"Reading the Prophetic stories in the Qur'an will enable you to develop a good understanding of the hardships and struggles the Prophets went through. This can be motivating for your hifdh journey."

TIP 157:
"You need to delve into the deeper meanings of the Qur'an. It is an ocean of knowledge. One will never be able to fully comprehend the beauty of this beautiful book."

TIP 158:
"No matter how much Arabic you learn or how much of the Qur'an you have understood, never assume that you know too much. Remember, we are always students of the Qur'an and Allah is our Teacher."

TIP 159:
"As you learn and understand the Qur'an more, there may be others who will contradict what you believe and fully deny its truth. Always reflect upon the second verse of Surah Baqarah: "This is a book about which there is no doubt.""

TIP 160:
"No matter how much of the Qur'an you have memorised, remember that you have a lifelong responsibility to not only retain your memory but to understand and implement the teachings of the Qur'an into your daily life."

TIP 161:
"Believe it or not, the intake of food and drink into your body has a strong effect on the memory of your Qur'an. Both are interlinked and play a significant role in the success of your hifdh journey."

MAINTAINING AN EFFECTIVE DIET, MEMORY AND REVISION METHODS

There are many methods of maintaining an effective and healthy diet. This section simply summarises the key diet methods, inspired by the sunnah as well as proven scientifically in our modern day and age.

Having a balanced eating routine can play a crucial role in developing a successful Qur'an memorisation journey. Mentally and physically you will feel more active and your mind will become more stimulated as a result. Your body will always need to be revitalised and energised.

Another important aspect of this section is the various memory retention and revision methods. Many hifdh students find it extremely difficult to maintain consistency in their learning but the honest truth is, you have to identify the learning method that suits you the most. Whether it's identifying the most suitable time of the day or using a specific type of Qur'an, it has to work for you and enable you to progress in your Qur'an memorisation journey.

Revision never stops, even for those who have memorised the entire Qur'an!

# WEEK TWENTY FOUR

TIP 162:
"Eating at sensible times and maintaining a balanced diet is essential in the productivity of your hifdh journey. Be disciplined in your daily intake of nutrition."

TIP 163:
"Scientific research shows that honey has immunity-boosting properties which works against memory loss. Consuming honey before going to sleep helps act as a fuel source for the brain and helps to preserve memory."

TIP 164:
"A new study has revealed that olive oil improves visual memory and verbal fluency. It can also lead to high scores in tests of memory, attention span and abstract thinking."

TIP 165:
"Figs are a phenomenal source of omega-3 and omega-6 fatty acids, which specifically helps the proper functioning of the brain system. Figs are also known as 'brain foods.'"

TIP 166:
"Recent studies have shown that pomegranates help you to enhance your memory through an increase in brain activity during verbal and memory testing.

TIP 167:
"Dates are a fantastic source of fibre which is extremely important for the brain. Fibre helps to slow down sugar absorption and regulates its supply, leading to enhanced memory function."

TIP 168:
"Scientists have found that those who have a grape-enriched diet benefited from increased metabolism in other areas of the brain, which showed improvements in memory performance."

WEEK TWENTY FIVE

TIP 169:
"Not only was black seed oil highly recommended by our Prophet Muhammad (PBUH) but scientific research has widely shown that those who consume black seed within their diet have enhanced their memory, attention and cognition."

TIP 170:
"For centuries, almonds have been one of the most recommended foods by Muslims for better memory. In particular, for Qur'an memorisation, scientific research has shown that almonds have a positive impact on the brain in that they boost one's memory."

TIP 171:
"Zam Zam water is a very beneficial source of intake and can provide miraculous cures for many who are suffering from health issues. If your memory is fading and you wish to improve your hifdh in general, drink Zam Zam water with a sincere intention."

TIP 172:
"Avocados are well-known for many health benefits, one being an increase in brain power. Science has proven that avocado is a brain food, so add it to your diet for increased memory and performance."

TIP 173:
"There is no specific oil to use when cooking food, especially whilst undertaking your hifdh journey. However, if you want to increase your brain potential, you should try using coconut oil instead. It has been proven to have a positive impact on brain activity."

TIP 174:
"The yolk is the most important part of an egg, as it contains most of the proteins and benefits. One of those benefits is improved brain performance. Include eggs in your daily diet to help ensure your Qur'an memory is alert and functional on a daily basis."

TIP 175:
"Science has proven that eating fish boosts your brainpower. In fact, scientists specifically recommend children to eat fish often to improve their memories."

WEEK TWENTY SIX

TIP 176:
"Not every brain enhancing food mentioned above may be suitable for you. But ensure you maintain a healthy diet which you can comfortably manage, and always be in firm control of your daily intake!"

TIP 177:
"Before starting your hifdh journey, you have to accept and understand that not everyone has a strong memory. Some may go through more challenges than others. Don't despair if your memory is weaker than others."

TIP 178:
"One method to improve your memory is by turning the pages of the Qur'an during your lesson recital for your teacher. In the long term, this will help you visualise the specific order of the pages of the Qur'an and boost your memory."

TIP 179:
"Constantly reciting the Qur'an from memory whilst commuting daily can help to strengthen your hifdh. This is especially true in the mornings when your mind is more alert and working faster."

TIP 180:
"Listening to the Qur'an is just as helpful, especially whilst undertaking your hifdh journey. Refresh your next day's lesson by listening to a portion recited by your chosen Qur'an reciter. You can listen and recite simultaneously!"

TIP 181:
"Reciting your daily lessons within your nafl prayers can really help to boost your memory. Select a specific portion to recite in each unit of prayer and make a daily or a weekly plan to stay on top of this. It can work wonders for your hifdh!"

TIP 182:
"Noting down in your Qur'an or on a separate notebook the mistakes/errors made whilst reciting new or revision lessons to your teacher is extremely essential. This helps you to reflect and improve your memory and helps to avoid making the same mistakes again!"

WEEK TWENTY SEVEN

TIP 183:
"Playing educational games which require memory skills can help to strengthen your memory retention. There are other productive methods of boosting your memory aside from reciting the Qur'an by heart."

TIP 184:
"Time management is a crucial element of having an effective memory. You must be disciplined in dedicating a good amount of time revisiting your Qur'an consistently each day. The success of your hifdh will mostly depend on how much time you spend learning outside the classes."

TIP 185:
"Mentally, you always need to be strong. There will be days when your self-esteem will be low and each new lesson will be challenging. Some days more than others. However, having the willpower to succeed despite the challenges is crucial!"

TIP 186:
"Keeping a written diary of how much Qur'an you have memorised on a short and long-term basis is very important. Reviewing the progress regularly can help to evaluate the strengths and weaknesses in your memory."

TIP 187:
"Maintaining a balanced sleeping routine weekly can help to keep your memory sharp and alert. Sleep is necessary to consolidate a memory (make it stick) so that it can be recalled in the future."

TIP 188:
"Focusing your mind solely on the lesson you are reciting to your teacher is a difficult and challenging task. Each day you will have many thoughts running through your mind. Controlling these thoughts is a huge factor in retaining a sharp and consistent memory."

TIP 189:
"Engaging in activities which require a huge amount of problem-solving skills can be an advantage for anyone undertaking their hifdh journey. Not only does this strengthen your memory but also allows your brain to think critically."

TIP 190:
"A very useful tool for hifdh revision is to regularly record the recital of your lesson and to review the recitation thereafter by playing back the recording. This is highly recommended and is particularly significant when revising individually in private."

TIP 191:
"Having a 'revision buddy' is a very helpful method for effective revision. Select a well-versed Qur'an reciter and someone you can trust. Plan regular revision sessions where you can both test each other and provide constructive feedback."

TIP 192:
"Do not overcommit yourself and burn out when it comes to hifdh revision. Plan a comfortable revision schedule that works for you, based on your daily routine."

TIP 193:
"The golden rule for revision is 'practice makes perfect.' Essentially, the more consistent you are in your revision, the more consistent you will be in progressing further with your hifdh journey."

TIP 194:
"Revision requires a lot of focus, discipline and commitment. Set aside your social life momentarily whilst you focus on your hifdh revision. Prioritise. Choose what is the most important and stick to it!"

TIP 195:
"Effective revision allows you to focus on your weaknesses and to turn them into strengths. If this can be achieved, then the revision has been successful."

TIP 196:
"One of the common mistakes hifdh students make is neglecting the long term revision. For example, if you have memorised 20 Juz, make a regular routine to revise the first 5 Juz and do not neglect them fully whilst focusing just on the short term revision!"

WEEK TWENTY NINE

TIP 197:
"Reciting the Qur'an and looking back inside it frequently is also a good form of hifdh revision. Especially when you have forgotten huge portions of a page and struggle to recite the page accurately with minimal hifdh errors."

TIP 198:
"One tried and tested technique employed in learning a new lesson is to break down the page into smaller chunks. You can choose how small the chunks are. Condensing the portions of a new lesson can help to maximise the memory retention."

TIP 199:
"Another effective memory retention method is to recite the new lesson while reading from the Qur'an several times before attempting to memorise the new lesson. It is important that you become familiar with the new lesson before memorising it."

TIP 200:
"There are specific words and verses in the Qur'an which are repeated frequently, more so than others. In Arabic, these are referred to as 'Mutashaabihaat'. If you learn the pattern of how they appear in the Qur'an, this can strengthen your memory."

TIP 201:
"One effective method to help you to learn your new lesson is by asking your teacher to recite the new lesson to you and for you to follow the recitation attentively from beginning to end."

TIP 202:
"Do not assume a certain lesson is easy or hard. Sometimes, you can become very complacent and neglect a certain Juz for example, because you felt it was easy to memorise at the time. Have a consistent approach to your revision by covering your previous lessons regularly."

TIP 203:
"The most important element of revision is consistency. No matter how small or large your revision lessons are, ensure that you are revising daily and do not neglect your revision at any cost. Always stay focused and disciplined."

SECTION SIX

UTILISING SUPPORT, RESOURCES AND TECHNOLOGY

One of the main purposes of including this section is to highlight the importance of seeking help and assistance. You must never be afraid to ask for support. Nowadays, we are very fortunate that support for hifdh can come in various forms. There is so much information available to us to access on a daily basis.

Resources which help you in your Qur'an memorisation journey should be utilised. There is nothing wrong in asking a close friend for some support or using online resources to assist you further in your hifdh. In fact, you should embrace technology and use it for the right means. We are surrounded by e-learning tools and the methods of learning through technology is advancing daily.

There are a range of tips provided in this section relating to technology, especially regarding the use of mobile apps. A key piece of advice is to always remember that your gadget can be a source of goodness or be your worst enemy, so choose your options carefully!

 WEEK THIRTY

TIP 204:
"Finding support to help you in your hifdh journey is not a bad thing. Support can come in many different forms: friends, family, teachers etc. You must choose the best method of support for you!"

TIP 205:
"You are not alone in your Qur'an memorisation journey. There are many people out there who will not hesitate to help you. Reach out to those who are the most sincere!"

TIP 206:
"Memorising the Qur'an is a very challenging task. Therefore, it is important that you seek support and advice; especially from those who have already memorised the Qur'an."

TIP 207:
"Parents and guardians play a crucial role in supporting you on your hifdh journey. Even by just relying on their support to wake you up in the morning for class, this will undoubtedly help you."

TIP 208:
"The support of your family is paramount to the outcome and success of your hifdh journey. If you can gain their unlimited support, you will find you have a more supportive and happier home."

TIP 209:
"There may be members of your family who have not been closely connected to the Qur'an. By gaining their support for your hifdh journey, this may bring them closer to this beautiful book."

TIP 210:
"Constantly keep those who support you in your prayers. Make it a daily habit to do so. You owe them that much at least."

✿ WEEK THIRTY ONE

TIP 211:
"In your darkest times, it is only the assistance of those who support you with sincerity that will be of benefit to you. Never forget and underestimate their input for your hifdh journey."

TIP 212:
"Form friendships with those who will not think twice about supporting you. Imagine having a wider circle of support, aside from your teachers and family members."

TIP 213:
"You should never feel too proud to ask for support. You cannot always do everything by yourself. Great minds think alike!

TIP 214:
"Imagine how many rewards will be gained from every single person who supports you throughout your hifdh journey. Their reward is with The Almighty, inshaAllah."

TIP 215:
There are many resources available online to help you in your hifdh journey. Utilise them and take advantage of them! Remember, there was a time when hardly any of these resources were available!"

TIP 216:
One effective online resource is YouTube. Listen to qualified and proficient Qur'an reciters regularly. Try to listen to your favourite reciter while simultaneously revising your hifdh."

TIP 217:
There are hundreds of mobile apps which can help you in your Qur'an memorisation journey. Not every app is suited for your learning. Browse through and select the most appropriate app for you."

TIP 218:
"Another vital resource is to read books which offer tips and advice on how to improve your memory retention. There are many out there. Do some research and select the ones which help you the most!"

TIP 219:
"Taking part in online Qur'an quizzes will help to increase your knowledge. It will simultaneously help to boost your hifdh and enhance your confidence and motivation to succeed even more."

TIP 220:
"Having your own hifdh progress tracker helps to keep you organised and is a very good resource tool to use. Moreover, it allows you to personally track your progress on a short and long term basis."

TIP 221:
"You may be good at writing and you may enjoy reading. Why not create your own daily hifdh journal? Make a brief note of the daily struggles and achievements throughout your hifdh journey. It will inspire you and others!"

TIP 222:
"Furthermore, on YouTube there are several video clips of motivational speakers who offer words of advice on Qur'an memorisation. Utilise this and try and listen to as many as possible."

TIP 223:
"There are many short and long-term courses offered online to help you in your Qur'an memorisation. They are beneficial for people in all stages of their hifdh journey."

TIP 224:
"Many people benefit from Qur'ans that have colour coded rules for tajweed. This can be an effective resource to help you in reciting the Qur'an correctly."

WEEK THIRTY THREE

TIP 225:
"Using technology to help you in your Qur'an memorisation is very beneficial. Especially for those who travel frequently, where it is difficult to commit to a face-to-face class setting."

TIP 226:
"Many people utilise Skype to connect with qualified Qur'an teachers abroad. This is a very useful method to help you to stay on top of your tajweed and hifdh. It is flexible too, as you can schedule the classes around your own timetable."

TIP 227:
"Qur'an Companion is an excellent online resource tool. It provides a flexible learning environment that you can tailor to meet your learning style and preferences."

TIP 228:
The Tahfidh. Memorize. App is created and developed by the National Huffadh Association in the UK. It is an innovative new app which provides a range of tools and resources to support your hifdh journey."

TIP 229:
Qur'an Cube is a leading technology-based company which provides a range of electronic items to help you build a closer connection with the Qur'an. They sell their products worldwide."

TIP 230:
The Quran Challenge game is a really good and fun board game which you can play with your family and friends. This particular game will most definitely help to build your Qur'anic knowledge.

TIP 231:
The Quran Knowledge game is another interactive board game. The world of the Qur'an in one box is their motto. Available online throughout the world.

WEEK THIRTY FOUR

TIP 232:
The Quran Explorer game is a board game which is aimed at players aged eight and over. Again, an excellent opportunity to spend quality time with the family and to enhance your knowledge of the Qur'an!"

TIP 233:
The Quran Moon lamp is an excellent product aimed at growing your love and connection with the Qur'an. This product enables you to benefit from a range of Qur'an reciters with a remote control."

TIP 234:
The Tarteel app is amazing. You can simply recite any verse of the Qur'an and it will automatically detect your voice and display the specific verse with the English translation within the app!"

TIP 235:
"Quran Hive is another beneficial app, which allows you to type in a specific word or topic and in return, the app brings up the specific verses which relate to that specific word."

TIP 236:
Quran Memorisation (Hafiz) is a beneficial app which allows you to select the particular Surah or verse you want to memorise, and this app will play it on loop. You can specify the reciter and how many times you want the verses to repeat."

TIP 237:
If you are a frequent commuter, listening to the Qur'an on your device can really help you to progress your Qur'an memorisation. It allows you to utilise the time spent commuting and will strengthen your memory!"

TIP 238:
One very useful tool is for those who drive a vehicle, listening to the Qur'an and reciting at the same time is a very productive way of memorising the Qur'an. It allows you to learn the Qur'an in a comfortable and private space."

WEEK THIRTY FIVE

TIP 239:
"Downloading any app which helps you to learn Arabic is a huge advantage. This resource allows you to understand the Qur'an in your own time and will strengthen your connection with Allah."

TIP 240:
"One very useful method used in developing your Qur'an memorisation is by listening and watching the daily Taraweeh prayers from Makkah and Madinah. Have the Qur'an open in front of you or recite the Qur'an from memory as the Imam is reciting."

TIP 241:
Joining a WhatsApp or Telegram group focused on Qur'an memorisation can be an effective technology-based resource. Interacting with others and sharing hifdh tips and advice can be of huge benefit to you!"

TIP 242:
"Following trustworthy and credible social media accounts which share regular hifdh tips and advice is another technology-based resource which allows you to access regular resources to help you in your Qur'an memorisation."

TIP 243:
Your mobile phone is a very simple but powerful tool. Just by using your mobile phone device to record voice clips or make phone calls to a hifdh buddy, you can assist yourself in your Qur'an memorisation journey.

TIP 244:
Technology, apps and gadgets are not always a negative means. In fact, if you can utilise these tools to help build your knowledge of the Qur'an, it can prove to be a very positive method of strengthening your hifdh.

TIP 245:
"What is the first thing that you check on your mobile phone when you wake up in the morning? Social media? Email? Messages? Read or listen to the Qur'an first before doing so!"

RAMADAN HIFDH TIPS

Ramadan is the month in which the Qur'an was revealed. It is the key month in which we tend to recite the Qur'an more frequently than any other month. The tips within this section are designed to uplift and motivate you to maximise your time with the Qur'an in Ramadan.

There are many ways in which you can even prepare for a productive Ramadan. For example, you can build and increase your daily Qur'anic recitation from Sha'ban or Rajab, in an effort to be consistent by the time Ramadan comes around. The idea behind this is to prevent moments from slipping by or going to waste. Cherish every moment spent in this beautiful and blessed month.

Especially for those who lead the Taraweeh prayers, make a sincere attempt to learn the meanings of the Qur'an and try to understand what you are reciting in the Taraweeh prayers in particular and this should help you grow even closer to the Qur'an. Imagine if you may not live to see another Ramadan, would you not want to make this the best Ramadan ever?

Remember, it is not always about the quantity of Qur'an that you recite or memorise in Ramadan, rather it is about the quality of the Qur'an that has been instilled into your everyday life.

WEEK THIRTY SIX

TIP 246:
Cleanliness is one of the most important aspects in Islam. Especially for the one who is leading Salah, remaining in a clean state during the Salah is extremely essential, both inwardly and outwardly. ("Allah loves those who repent and keep themselves pure") (Qur'an 2:222)

TIP 247:
Establish a more rigorous daily routine, especially from Sha'baan, where you are focused on refreshing your daily hifdh. A recommended amount to revise daily is 1 - 3 Juz. Keep it consistent!

TIP 248:
A hafidh can develop a closer relationship with the Qur'an if he understands what he is reading. A good routine would be to read an English translation of the verses that you will be reciting within Taraweeh for each night. "Will they not then ponder the Qur'an or are there locks upon their hearts?" [Qur'an 47:24]

TIP 249:
Tajweed always takes precedence over speed and voice. There is no speed limit when you recite the Qur'an! Recite in a calm, composed and clear tone with a consistent and preferably medium pace of recitation.

TIP 250:
Ask Allah daily to help you with your Taraweeh preparation. There are many important du'as which can be taken from The Qur'an to help you throughout Taraweeh. Verses 25 - 28 of Surah TaHa are extremely helpful and beneficial to recite just before you stand on the musalla. It can calm nerves as well.

TIP 251:
As a hafidh in Ramadan, especially if you will be leading the Taraweeh prayers, it is wise not to 'overeat' during Iftaar, as you will struggle to recite during the Taraweeh prayers. Have a balanced and controlled healthy/nutritious diet, where you consume plenty of vegetables and fruit. Drinking black tea with honey or lukewarm water prior to leaving your home for Taraweeh prayers also helps the throat.

TIP 252:
Particularly during the month of Ramadan, establish a hifdh buddy. Someone who is committed to helping you and who can listen to your Qur'an each day in preparation for the Taraweeh prayers. Many huffadh have admitted that having an extra ear to listen over their Qur'an is extremely helpful and can help to strengthen their hifdh as well as highlight errors and improvements that need to be made.

WEEK THIRTY SEVEN

TIP 253:
It is not an easy feat, to stand on a musalla and lead the Taraweeh prayers. It is courageous and one of the most challenging acts you will ever undertake in your life. No matter how many times you lead the Taraweeh prayers, those nerves and anxious feelings will never go away! Be strong and brave, and remember, it is Allah who has put you there on the Musalla!

TIP 254:
There is no such thing as a perfect hafidh! You are still human and prone to making some mistakes now and again. One of the best ways to improve your recitation and hifdh is to record your portion of the Taraweeh prayers and listen back to it each day. Critically listen to your recitation and aim to improve it. Remember, there is always room for improvement!

TIP 255:
Understanding the Arabic language can really help to strengthen one's hifdh. It's not just about memorising but rather understanding what Allah is saying in the Qur'an.

TIP 256:
Being a hafidh of one Surah, Juz or the entire Qur'an is not just about what you have memorised but 'preserving' what you have learnt and acting upon it. The word 'hafidh' doesn't just mean to memorise but to also protect and preserve this Glorious Book.

TIP 257:
Don't tell people how much of the Qur'an you have memorised. Let them see the beauty of the Qur'an in your actions. It isn't about how far you've reached in the Qur'an but how far The Qur'an has reached in you.

TIP 258:
Pick any time. Any hour-day or night-your choice. A time that's convenient for you. A time that suits you the most. But don't ever say it's too late or there's not enough time. Remember, there's no age barrier to hifdh and it is never too late to memorise the Qur'an!

TIP 259:
Spend less time on your mobile phone and more time with the Qur'an. A student once asked his teacher: "How was the Sahabah's relationship with the Qur'an?" He replied: "Like your relationship now with your mobile phone!"

 # WEEK THIRTY EIGHT

TIP 260:
What is the character of a hafidh?
"A memoriser of the Qur'an should be known for his long night prayers when people are asleep, his fasting when people are eating, his sadness when people are happy, his silence when people are talking nonsense, and his humbleness when people are not. He should be wise, gentle and not talk too much; he should not be rude, negligent, clamorous nor hot tempered." - Ibn Mas'ud

TIP 261:
Practice your hifdh frequently during salah. Plan a daily schedule of how much Qur'an you will recite in your fardh, sunnah or nafl prayers. Try it and see how effective this method can be.

TIP 262:
Being a hafidh is a lifelong responsibility.
"The memoriser of the Qur'an carries the flag of Islam. He shouldn't waste his time in vain amusement, distractions and pointless matters with those who do so, out of respect for the Qur'an." - Al-Fudayl bin 'Iyad

TIP 263:
"When you are becoming a hafidh, you will face hardships. At times, you may feel like giving up completely. Persevere and try your hardest. Remember, Allah only chooses specific servants of His to memorise the Qur'an. One of them is you, inshaAllah!

TIP 264:
"Nowadays the Qur'an is being 'mutilated' by our huffadh in Taraweeh prayers. There is a lack of care taken for tajweed and correct pronunciation. This is wrong and against the laws of the Qur'an. Qiraa'ah should never be compromised over speed!" - Qari Ayoob Essack (Hafidhahullah)

TIP 265:
The easiest part is to memorise a new verse from scratch. It builds excitement and increases the desire to memorise more. But the hardest task is to retain what you have memorised every day until the end of your life. That is the ultimate task for a hafidh.

TIP 266:
The amount of respect you receive from people because of what you have memorised is beautiful. But remember, it is all from Allah. Stay humble. Do not let pride overtake you. Never think that you are better than others just because you are a hafidh.

 # WEEK THIRTY NINE

TIP 267:

"Do not scatter the Qur'an like inferior dates and do not chant it quickly as with poetry. Stop and marvel at its wonders, move hearts with it and do not let your concern be the end of the Surah."

- Abdullah ibn Mas'ud (RA)

TIP 268:

The beauty of the Qur'an is that every verse hits you differently, depending on what is going on in your life at that time. It always applies. Always. Pause. Reflect. Take heed.

TIP 269:

The Qur'an should be your best friend. Nothing can come close to your relationship with the Qur'an. It should calm you down whenever you are sad. There is something about the Qur'an once it enters your heart and takes away any worldly negativity. It is indescribable.

TIP 270:

Even if you have memorised a few verses, Surahs or a Juz of the Qur'an. You've already won. Now go live your entire life according to these verses you have memorized. One of the responsibilities of a hafidh is to act upon what you have learnt.

TIP 271:

The Qur'an is unlike any other book. It is the most memorised book on the planet. You can never master the Qur'an. It masters you. It supersedes. It's not superseded upon. It imposes. It's not imposed upon.

TIP 272:

When you have gained the status of a hafidh, never think you have mastered the Qur'an. Always consider yourself to be a student. Humility and sincerity is key. Remain in the service of the Qur'an for as long as you live and inshaAllah you will reap the rewards in Jannah.

TIP 273:

There are people in their graves who wished they had either memorised the Qur'an or gained a closer relationship with it. For as long as you are alive, value and appreciate what Allah has blessed you with. Remember, not every person can become a hafidh. Allah chooses whom He wishes specifically.

 # WEEK FORTY

TIP 274:
The task of a hafidh is not just to pick up and read the Qur'an in Ramadan only. Rather it is a lifelong responsibility. 365 days a year. Read as much as you can daily. Create a fixed timetable that suits you best. Don't let Shaitaan distract you. Never let a day go past where you do not refresh your hifdh.

TIP 275:
Try and commit to a daily Qur'an recitation schedule during Ramadan. Choose a suitable routine adapted to your schedule. Make it consistent for the entire month of Ramadan.

TIP 276:
A useful method of refreshing your hifdh during Ramadan is by following the verses recited by the Imam during the Taraweeh prayers. Continue this until you have exceeded the portions you have memorised."

TIP 277:
"One of the best times in the day for memorising the Qur'an is in the early hours of the morning. Dedicate some time before or after suhoor for some hifdh learning and revision.

TIP 278:
Increase the amount of Qur'an that you usually recite daily in the month of Ramadan. For example, if you already have a daily routine of reciting 1 Juz, then try to read more than this amount daily in Ramadan especially.

TIP 279:
If you can, never miss the opportunity to lead the Taraweeh prayers during Ramadan. You'll be amazed at how strong your hifdh becomes once you have taken up this opportunity."

TIP 280:
Ramadan is the month of the Qur'an. It is not befitting if you do not maximise the recitation of the Qur'an throughout this blessed month. Make every moment count!

QUR'ANIC DU'AS

The Qur'an is full of words of wisdom and guidance for us all. However, this section contains carefully selected supplications from the Qur'an to help you in attaining a closer connection to Allah during your Qur'an memorisation journey.

This selection of 30 Qur'anic du'as are included to grant you the opportunity to learn and memorise some of these beautiful supplications. Asking The Almighty for help and guidance is the best form of support one can rely on, especially when memorising the Qur'an. In fact, you will have probably recited many of these verses within your revision but not have been aware that these are indeed very beneficial supplications.

You should always make a habit of asking Allah for help daily. The task of memorising the Qur'an is not easy at all. It requires a lot dedication, strength and motivation. This can only come from Allah. Yes, if you put in a lot of hard work and effort, inshaAllah you will see positive results but ultimately it is Allah who decides whether or not you can progress.

Remember, du'a is the most powerful weapon for a believer.

✸ WEEK FORTY ONE

TIP 281:
Our Lord! Grant us good in this world and good in the life to come and keep us safe from the torment of the Fire (2:201)

TIP 282:
Our Lord! Bestow on us endurance and make our foothold sure and give us help against those who reject faith. (2:250)

TIP 283:
Our Lord! Take us not to task if we forget or fall into error. (2:286)

TIP 284:
Our Lord! Lay not upon us such a burden as You did lay upon those before us. (2:286)

TIP 285:
Our Lord! Impose not on us that which we have not the strength to bear, grant us forgiveness and have mercy on us. You are our Protector. Help us against those who deny the truth. (2:286)

TIP 286:
Our Lord! Let not our hearts deviate from the truth after You have guided us, and bestow upon us mercy from Your grace. Verily You are the Giver of bounties without measure. (3:8)

TIP 287:
Our Lord! Forgive us our sins and the lack of moderation in our doings, and make firm our steps and succour us against those who deny the truth. (3:147)

* An arabic copy of the following verses are noted at the back

✦ WEEK FORTY TWO

TIP 288:
Our Lord, accept [this] from us. Indeed You are the Hearing, the Knowing. (2:127)

TIP 289:
Our Lord! Whomsoever You shall commit to the Fire, truly You have brought [him] to disgrace, and never will wrongdoers find any helpers (3:192)

TIP 290:
Our Lord! Behold we have heard a voice calling us unto faith: "Believe in your Lord" and we have believed. (3:193)

TIP 291:
Our Lord! Forgive us our sins and efface our bad deeds and take our souls in the company of the righteous. (3:193)

TIP 292:
Our Lord! And grant us that which you have promised to us by Your messengers and save us from shame on the Day of Judgement. Verily You never fail to fulfil Your promise. (3:194)

TIP 293:
Our Lord! We have sinned against ourselves, and unless You grant us forgiveness and bestow Your mercy upon us, we shall most certainly be lost! (7:23)

TIP 294:
Our Lord! Place us not among the people who have been guilty of evildoing. (7:47)

* An arabic copy of the following verses are noted at the back

TIP 295:
Our Lord! Lay open the truth between us and our people, for You are the best of all to lay open the truth. (7:89)

TIP 296:
Our Lord! Pour out on us patience and constancy, and make us die as those who have surrendered themselves unto You. (7:126)

TIP 297:
Our Lord! Make us not a trial for the evildoing folk, and save as by Your mercy from people who deny the truth (10:85-86)

TIP 298:
Our Lord! You truly know all that we may hide [in our hearts] as well as all that we bring into the open, for nothing whatever, be it on earth or in heaven, remains hidden from Allah (14:38)

TIP 299:
Our Lord! Bestow on us mercy from Your presence and dispose of our affairs for us in the right way. (18:10)

TIP 300:
Our Lord! Grant that our spouses and our offspring be a comfort to our eyes, and give us the grace to lead those who are conscious of You. (25:74)

TIP 301:
Our Lord! You embrace all things within Your Grace and Knowledge, forgive those who repent and follow Your path, and ward off from them the punishment of Hell. (40:7)

* An arabic copy of the following verses are noted at the back

✦ WEEK FORTY FOUR

TIP 302:
Our Lord! Make them enter the Garden of Eden which You have promised to them, and to the righteous from among their fathers, their wives and their offspring, for verily You are alone the Almighty and the truly Wise. (40:8)

TIP 303:
Our Lord! Relieve us of the torment, for we do really believe. (44:12)

TIP 304:
Our Lord! Forgive us our sins as well as those of our brethren who proceeded us in faith and let not our hearts entertain any unworthy thoughts or feelings against [any of] those who have believed. Our Lord! You are indeed full of kindness and Most Merciful (59:10)

TIP 305:
Our Lord! In You we have placed our trust, and to You do we turn in repentance, for unto You is the end of all journeys. (60:4)

TIP 306:
Our Lord! Perfect our light for us and forgive us our sins, for verily You have power over all things. (66:8)

TIP 307:
Our Lord! Make of us Muslims, bowing to Thy (Will), and of our progeny a people Muslim, bowing to Thy (will); and show us our place for the celebration of (due) rites; and turn unto us (in Mercy); for Thou art the Oft-Returning, Most Merciful (2:128)

TIP 308:
Our Lord! Bestow on us Mercy from Thyself, and dispose of our affair for us in the right way! (18:10)

---

* An arabic copy of the following verses are noted at the back

✦ WEEK FORTY FIVE

TIP 309:
"Our Lord! Grant us that which You have promised to us through Your Apostles and disgrace us not on the Day of Reckoning. Surely You never fail in Your Promise." (3:194)

TIP 310:
"O our Lord! Forgive me and my parents and all the Muslims on the Day when Reckoning will take place. (14:41)

TIP 311:
"O Allah: Lord and Cherisher of us all! Send down to us a tray of food from heaven, that it may become a day of rejoicing for all of us and (let it be) a Sign from You; and grant us sustenance and indeed You are the Best Provider of all." (5:114)

* An arabic copy of the following verses are noted at the back

LIFE AFTER MEMORISING THE QUR'AN

This final section of the book is arguably the most important part of your Qur'an memorisation journey. It reminds you that the learning journey is never over. In fact, becoming a hafidh or hafidhah is a lifelong commitment. You must make time every day to revise and learn your hifdh until the day you depart from this world. This responsibility is to be taken seriously.

Additionally, one of the key reasons as to why this section has been included within this book is to motivate and encourage those who have maybe forgotten or not revisited their hifdh for a while. This happens to a lot of us, especially when we neglect our daily routine in revising our Qur'an. Furthermore, it is never too late to turn to the Qur'an. If Allah has blessed you initially to memorise the Qur'an, then surely He can bless you by enabling you to retain the memory of the Qur'an within you.

Life after memorising the Qur'an is not easy. In fact, being a hafidh or a hafidhah is arguably more challenging than the journey of becoming one. One of the most challenging aspects of maintaining your revision of the Qur'an is remaining strong in your memory retention, especially as you get older. Naturally, your memory will gradually become weaker as your age increases but inshaAllah the more consistent you are in your daily revision of the Qur'an, the stronger your memory will remain.

Always keep the Qur'an a focal point of your life. Be disciplined in making time daily for your Qur'anic revision. Never let a day go past where you do not revisit the Qur'an.

TIP 312:
You have spent days, months and maybe even years in memorising the entire Qur'an. Now you have the lifelong responsibility to practice what you have memorised."

TIP 313:
"Become a person of the Qur'an. Adopt a humble, soft and loveable approach. Speak to people with love, mercy and wisdom. This is befitting of a hafidh/hafidhah."

TIP 314:
"Never assume that you 'know it all.' You have a long way to go. Just memorising the Qur'an is the beginning of a fruitful and everlasting journey."

TIP 315:
"Try to give back to the community. Try and volunteer some time and help out in the mosque or institution where you had completed your hifdh."

✦ WEEK FORTY SIX

TIP 316:
"The Prophet Muhammad (PBUH) said: The best of you are those who learn and teach the Qur'an." Why not set some time aside and teach the Qur'an in your local community?"

TIP 317:
"Always be punctual in leading the Taraweeh prayers, especially after completing your Qur'an memorisation. This will especially help to retain your memory year after year."

TIP 318:
"The Qur'an should always remain a focal point of your life. Your entire day should begin and end with the recitation of the Qur'an. This will bring a lot of barakah into your daily routine."

TIP 319:
"Always strive to improve your recitation and Tajweed. Seek opportunities to learn advanced Qur'an classes to enhance your connection with the Qur'an."

TIP 320:
"If you have memorised the entire Qur'an but have not made an attempt to learn Arabic, seize the opportunity. If Allah has helped you to become a hafidh/hafidhah, surely He can help you to learn the Arabic language?"

TIP 321:
Do not be fazed or starstruck with the title of 'hafidh' or 'hafidhah'. These are just statuses which people attribute your name to. It should not make you proud or arrogant."

TIP 322:
"Maintain a daily routine to refresh and learn your revision. Never let a day go past in which you do not revise your Qur'an memorisation."

TIP 323:
"Do not lose contact with your teachers. They are the ones who have helped you to memorise the Qur'an. Always make a habit of visiting them and never forget them in your supplications."

TIP 324:
"The supplication of your teachers is priceless. It may be the case that their constant supplications for you during your hifdh journey were a significant factor in you attaining the title of a hafidh or a hafidhah!"

TIP 325:
"The love you have for your parents or guardians should amount to the same love that you have for your teachers. They deserve the same amount of love, respect and honour."

TIP 326:
"Allah has gifted you with the title of a hafidh or a hafidhah. Do not let a day go past whereby you do not thank and appreciate Allah's enormous blessings of this gift."

TIP 327:
"You have completed your Qur'an memorisation journey. But there are many around the world who struggle daily and are finding the hifdh journey extremely strenuous and challenging. Spare a prayer for them in your supplications."

TIP 328:
"Your parents or guardians may have supported and encouraged you the most in your Qur'an memorisation journey. Thank them and pray for them daily!"

TIP 329:
"You have spent a lot of time memorising the Qur'an. Now utilise your time finding out about the history of the Qur'an. How was it revealed and compiled? What are the stories behind the chapters and verses? There is so much to learn!"

WEEK FORTY EIGHT

TIP 330:
"It is wise to try and spend some extra time refreshing your hifdh within your Qur'an memorisation class after you have completed your hifdh journey. It will benefit you in the long run."

TIP 331:
"Do not fall into the trap of distancing yourself away from the Qur'an. You may choose to no longer be in the classroom environment but remember you are always facing a test from Allah daily! Try to pass each one."

TIP 332:
"Ease is the biggest threat to progress. Do not become lazy or complacent in your Qur'an revision, especially after completing your hifdh. Progress and develop by learning more about this beautiful book."

TIP 333:
"It is not unusual for your hifdh to become weaker as you get older. Your memory does fade away slowly but the more you revise your Qur'an daily, the stronger it will always remain."

TIP 334:
"Never be scared to ask for help. Even if it means by going back to visit your teachers. Always have an open and transparent relationship with your teachers. Their wisdom and guidance is priceless."

TIP 335:
"You will face hardships daily in life and some days may be more difficult than others. The Qur'an will be your source of comfort and solace. Hold on to this beautiful book and seek refuge in Allah."

TIP 336:
"Temptation is always around you especially that you are now free to select your own hifdh revision routine. You may no longer have a hifdh class to attend. Discipline your nafs and commit to a daily routine."

WEEK FORTY NINE

TIP 337:
"Never assume that you are a teacher of the Qur'an. You will never inherit the 'master' or the 'expert' of the Qur'an. Always assume that you are a student and Allah is the Teacher."

TIP 338:
"Due to your rigorous Qur'an memorisation routine whilst you were undertaking your hifdh journey, you may not have been able to focus on your family as much. Regain the time and spend quality family time regularly."

TIP 339:
"Treat your hifdh revision like Salah. The same way in which you are obliged to pray five times daily, see it as an obligation to commit to your hifdh revision daily. Seven days a week. No ifs or buts."

TIP 340:
"One of the most challenging aspects of being a hafidh is making time daily to refresh your Qur'an memorisation. You are in control of your own daily routine. Do not over commit and stick to realistic daily routines."

TIP 341:
"Give yourself a target of how many completions of the Qur'an you will aim to do in each month. Keep a progress tracker and review your progress."

TIP 342:
"Hifdh is not about quantity but quality. Do not attempt to read a huge portion of the Qur'an daily as you may make several mistakes in your hifdh at the same time. Focus on condensed portions and minimise the mistakes made."

TIP 343:
"Always remind yourself that the learning never stops. You will never 'master' the entire Qur'an as this book is an ocean of knowledge. Try to learn something new every day."

WEEK FIFTY

TIP 344:
"Socialising and interacting with other huffadh or hafidhaat is very important. Form a close circle of friends who have memorised the Qur'an and share tips and advice on how you are maintaining the revision of your hifdh."

TIP 345:
"Initiate a deeper love for the Qur'an at home. Encourage your family members to join you in a Qur'an circle (Halaqah). It could be just reading inspirational stories from the Qur'an or reciting selected verses from the Qur'an regularly. This will develop a closer family bond too."

TIP 346:
"No matter how far you progress in terms of your academic or career route. The Qur'an always comes first. Barakah, success and contentment will not be attained without maintaining a daily connection with the Qur'an."

TIP 347:
"One effective method to maintain the strength of your hifdh is by entering Qur'an competitions, either locally, nationally or globally. This can motivate and encourage you to strengthen your hifdh even more."

TIP 348:
"Never let Shaitaan deceive you. After completing your hifdh, hard times may arise. You could be faced with huge tests. Do not forego the Qur'an as a result. Hold onto the Qur'an and do not let go!"

TIP 349:
"One effective tool of strengthening your hifdh is by underlining or circling specific hifdh errors made within your Mushaf. This is to ensure that you do not keep on making the same hifdh mistakes you used to make whilst you were in your hifdh journey."

TIP 350:
"You may feel frustrated and tired. You are making lots of hifdh mistakes, even after completing the entire Qur'an memorisation. Do not panic! Take a deep breath and revisit the mistake again and again. Remind yourself that you are not perfect!"

✺ WEEK FIFTY ONE

TIP 351:
"Believe it or not, even the Imams of the biggest mosques in the world make hifdh mistakes during the prayers. No matter how small or large the congregation is, you will always be prone to some mistakes. Learn from them!"

TIP 352:
"Understanding the Qur'an is a challenging task. It takes years of committed learning. It is not an overnight task by any means. Take small steps in understanding this beautiful book and see how your relationship with Allah develops."

TIP 353:
"One lifelong goal for a hafidh or hafidhah is to change your character or personality for the better. The Qur'an should be your personality. People should think of the Qur'an when they interact with you."

TIP 354:
"As a hafidh or hafidhah, if you are consistent in doing acts which He likes, then in return He will be consistent in granting you your wishes and prayers, inshaAllah."

TIP 355:
"Always remind yourself, when you commenced your hifdh journey, it was a lifelong commitment you had made with Allah that you will protect and preserve the Qur'an."

TIP 356:
"As a hafidh or a hafidhah, you should always be aware that there will be a day in which The Almighty will question you in relation to your connection with the Qur'an. Will the Qur'an be a witness for you or against you?"

TIP 357:
"Don't just become used to reciting the Qur'an from memory. Make it a habit to regularly recite the Qur'an by looking into the Mushaf too. This is an effective method for memory retention."

WEEK FIFTY TWO

TIP 358:
"There is always room for improvement. You are not perfect. Whether it is your hifdh, voice or Tajweed. Keep on practicing daily and try to improve as much as you can!"

TIP 359:
"One common aspect of many Qur'an recitations by a hafidh or Hafidhah, is that they tend to imitate other well-known reciters of the Qur'an. However, try and be unique and work hard to develop your own style of recitation."

TIP 360:
"It is easy to simply recite the smaller chapters from Juz 'Amma during our five times prayers. However, one effective method is to recite from random sections of the Qur'an during your prayers. This will help to strengthen your hifdh."

TIP 361:
"The term 'hafidh' or 'hafidhah' is not something to be taken lightly. Understand and value the meaning of these words. You have to implement this into your daily life."

TIP 362:
"Never look down at someone who is memorising the Qur'an or see yourself as someone superior. Remember, you were once in their shoes and struggling to memorise the Qur'an."

TIP 363:
"Be loyal to the Qur'an always. Cherish and appreciate the value of this book. Make it your daily dose of motivation always!"

TIP 364:
"Make it a lifelong aim to always be in the service of the Qur'an. Even after you pass away, let it be that people remember you as the one who loved the Qur'an!"

TIP 365:
"This is the easiest part, memorising the Qur'an. The hardest part is when you complete memorising the entire Qur'an. Because then it becomes your lifelong responsibility to retain every single letter that you have memorised until the day you depart from this world."

365 TIPS

TO HELP YOU MEMORISE THE QUR'AN
'ONE MOTIVATIONAL TIP FOR EACH DAY OF THE YEAR'

REFERENCES

TIP 41 (AL TABARI, AL TAFSIR 1:80)

عن شقيق عن ابن مسعود رضي الله عنه : كان الرجل منا إذا تعلم عشر آيات لم يجاوزهن حتى يعرف معانيهن والعمل بهن

TIP 42 (BUKHARI 5027 , ABU DAWUD 1352 & TIRMIDHI 290)

عن عثمان بن عفان رضي الله عنه قال : قال رسول الله ﷺ : خيركم من تعلم القرآن وعلمه
ولفظ الترمذي 'خيركم أو أفضلكم

TIP 43 (IBN AL JAWZEE, SIFAAT AS-SAFWA PAGE 111)

عن المسيب بن رافع عن عبد الله بن مسعود قال: ينبغي لحامل القرآن أن يعرف بليله إذا الناس نائمون، وبنهاره إذا الناس مفطرون، وبحزنه إذا الناس فرحون وبكائه إذا الناس يضحكون وبصمته إذا الناس يخلطون وخشوعه إذا الناس يختالون وينبغي لحامل القرآن أن يكون باكيا محزونا حليما حكيما سكيتا ولا ينبغي لحامل القرآن أن يكون جافيا ولا غافلا ولا سخابا ولا صياحا ولا حديدا

TIP 44 (AL BUKHARI 4937 & MUSLIM 797)

عن عائشة رضي الله عنها: قالت: قال رسول الله ﷺ: الذي يقرأ القرآن وهو ماهر به مع السفرة الكرام البررة، والذي يقرأ القرآن ويتتعتع فيه وهو عليه شاق له أجران رواه [مسلم، 798، واللفظ له] و [البخاري، 4937 ولفظه 'مثل الذي يقرأ القرآن وهو حافظ له مع السفرة الكرام البررة، ومثل الذي يقرأ ويتعاهده وهو عليه شديد فله أجران

TIP 45 (SHU'AB AL-IMAN 1:407)

عن ابن مسعود رضي الله عنه: لا تهذوا القرآن هذ الشعر ولا تنثروه نثر الدقل وقفوا عند عجائبه وحركوا به القلوب وأيضا: بإسناده حدثنا الزعفراني حدثنا شبابة عن المغيرة عن حمزة عن أبي إبراهيم قال: قال عبد الله: أقرؤوا القرآن حركوا به القلوب ولا يكون هم أحدكم آخر السورة

365 TIPS

TO HELP YOU MEMORISE THE QUR'AN
'ONE MOTIVATIONAL TIP FOR EACH DAY OF THE YEAR'

REFERENCES

TIP 46 (HILYAH AL-AWLIYAH 8:92)

قال فضيل بن عياض رحمه الله: حامل القرآن حامل راية الإسلام، لا ينبغي له أن يلغو مع من يلغو ولا أن يلهو مع من يلهو ولا يسهو مع من يسهو وينبغي لحامل القرآن أن لا يكون له إلى الخلق حاجة لا إلى الخلفاء فمن دونهم وينبغي أن يكون حوايج الخلق إليه

TIP 47 (IQTIDAA AL-ILM AL-AMAL, PAGE 71)

قال عمر بن الخطاب رضي الله عنه: لا يغررركم من قرأ لكم القرآن إنما هو كلام نتكلم به ولكن انظروا من يعمل به

TIP 48 (QUR'AN 54:22)

وَلَقَدْ يَسَّرْنَا الْقُرْآنَ لِلذِّكْرِ فَهَلْ مِن مُّدَّكِرٍ - 54:22

TIP 49 (NARRATED BY AL-TIRMIDHI 2514)

عن عبد الله بن عمرو بن العاص رضي الله عنه: عن النبي ﷺ قال: يقال لصاحب القرآن: اقرأ وارتق ورتل كما كنت ترتل في الدنيا، فإن منزلتك عند آخر آية تقرؤها

TIP 50 (AL MADKHAL ILA AS SUNAN PAGE 325, HILYAH AL-AWLIYAH 9:123)

قال الإمام الشافعي رحمه الله: ليس العلم ما حفظ، العلم ما نفع

TIP 51 (AYYUHAL WALAD, PAGE 25)

في كتاب الإمام الغزالي رحمه الله: العلم بلا عمل جنون والعمل بلا علم لا يكون

365 TIPS

TO HELP YOU MEMORISE THE QUR'AN
'ONE MOTIVATIONAL TIP FOR EACH DAY OF THE YEAR'

REFERENCES

TIP 53 (MUSNAD AHMAD, 25813)

عن الحسن ، قال : سألت عائشة عن خلق رسول الله - صلى الله عليه وسلم - فقالت : كان خلقه القرآن

TIP 54 (HAKIM, 319)

عن أبي هريرة رضى الله عنه قال : قال رسول الله - صلى الله عليه وسلم -إني قد تركت فيكم شيئين لن تضلوا بعدهما: كتاب الله وسنتي، ولن يتفرقا حتى يردا على الحوض

TIP 61 (ZAAD AL-MA'AD IBN AL QAYYIM PAGE 108)

قال ابن القيم الجوزية : ولهذا كان أهل القرآن هم العالمون به والعاملون به وان لم يحفظوه عن ظهر قلب

TIP 62 (IBN MAJAH 216, TIRMIDHI 2905)

عن علي بن أبي طالب رضي الله عنه قال : قال رسول الله - صلى الله عليه وسلم - من قرأ القران وحفظه أدخله الله الجنة وشفعه في عشرة من أهل بيته كلهم قد استوجبوا النار

TIP 65 (MA'ARIFAH AL-QURRA AL-KIBAAR PAGE 125)

قال سويد بن عبد العزيز : كان أبو الدرداء إذا صلى الغداة في جامع دمشق، اجتمع الناس للقراءة عليه ، فكان يجعلهم عشرة عشرة، وعلى كل عشرة عريفا، ويقف هو في المحراب يرمقهم ببصره فإذا غلط أحد رجع إلى عريفه، فاذا غلط عريف رجع إلى أبي الدرداء فسأله عن ذلك

TIP 66 (MARIFAT AL-QURRA AL-KIBAAR PAGE 125)

عن مسلم بن مشكم قال : قال لي أبو الدرداء رضي الله عنه : اعدد لي من يقرأ عندي القرآن . فعددتهم ألفا وستمائة ونيفا. وكان لكل عشرة منهم مقرئ وكان أبو الدرداء يطوف عليهم قائمًا، فإذا أحكم الرجل منهم يعني حفظ القرآن ، حول إلى أبي الدرداء

365 TIPS

TO HELP YOU MEMORISE THE QUR'AN
'ONE MOTIVATIONAL TIP FOR EACH DAY OF THE YEAR'

REFERENCES

TIP 67 (TABARI 1:80)

عن أبي عبد الرحمان السلمي: حدثنا الذين كانوا يقرئوننا أنهم كانوا يستقرئون من النبي ﷺ فكانوا إذا تعلّموا عشر آيات لم يخلّفوها حتى يعلموا بما فيها من العمل فتعلمنا القرآن والعمل جميعا

TIP 69 (BUKHARI 6465 & MUSLIM 783)

عن عائشة رضي الله عنها قالت قال رسول الله ﷺ أحب الأعمال إلى الله أدومها وإن قلّ وكانت عائشة إذا عملت العمل لزمته

TIP 70 ('ALI RA)

قال علي بن أبي طالب رضي الله عنه: لا جمال أزين من العقل

TIP 73 (MUSLIM 804)

عن أبي أمامة الباهلي رضي الله عنه قال: سمعت رسول الله ﷺ يقول اقرؤوا القرآن فإنه يأتي يوم القيامة شفيعا لأصحابه

TIP 75 (TIRMIDHI, 6910)

عن ابن مسعود رضي الله عنه قال: قال رسول الله ﷺ من قرأ حرفا من كتاب الله فله حسنة، والحسنة بعشر أمثالها لا أقول 'الم' حرف ولكن ألف حرف ولام حرف وميم حرف

TIP 76 (TIRMIDHI 2887)

عن أنس رضي الله عنه قال: قال النبي ﷺ: إن لكل شيء قلبا وقلب القرآن يس ومن قرأ يس كتب الله له بقرائتها قراءة القرآن عشر مرات

365 TIPS

TO HELP YOU MEMORISE THE QUR'AN
'ONE MOTIVATIONAL TIP FOR EACH DAY OF THE YEAR'

REFERENCES

TIP 281 رَبَّنَا آتِنَا فِي الدُّنْيَا حَسَنَةً وَفِي الْآخِرَةِ حَسَنَةً وَقِنَا عَذَابَ النَّارِ - 2:201

TIP 282 رَبَّنَا أَفْرِغْ عَلَيْنَا صَبْرًا وَثَبِّتْ أَقْدَامَنَا وَانصُرْنَا عَلَى الْقَوْمِ الْكَافِرِينَ - 2:250

TIP 283 رَبَّنَا لَا تُؤَاخِذْنَا إِن نَّسِينَا أَوْ أَخْطَأْنَا - 2:286

TIP 284 رَبَّنَا وَلَا تَحْمِلْ عَلَيْنَا إِصْرًا كَمَا حَمَلْتَهُ عَلَى الَّذِينَ مِن قَبْلِنَا - 2:286

TIP 285 رَبَّنَا وَلَا تُحَمِّلْنَا مَا لَا طَاقَةَ لَنَا بِهِ وَاعْفُ عَنَّا وَاغْفِرْ لَنَا وَارْحَمْنَا أَنتَ مَوْلَانَا فَانصُرْنَا عَلَى الْقَوْمِ الْكَافِرِينَ - 2:286

TIP 286 رَبَّنَا لَا تُزِغْ قُلُوبَنَا بَعْدَ إِذْ هَدَيْتَنَا وَهَبْ لَنَا مِن لَّدُنكَ رَحْمَةً إِنَّكَ أَنتَ الْوَهَّابُ - 3:8

TIP 287 رَبَّنَا اغْفِرْ لَنَا ذُنُوبَنَا وَإِسْرَافَنَا فِي أَمْرِنَا وَثَبِّتْ أَقْدَامَنَا وَانصُرْنَا عَلَى الْقَوْمِ الْكَافِرِينَ - 3:147

TIP 288 رَبَّنَا تَقَبَّلْ مِنَّا إِنَّكَ أَنتَ السَّمِيعُ الْعَلِيمُ - 2:127

TIP 289 رَبَّنَا إِنَّكَ مَن تُدْخِلِ النَّارَ فَقَدْ أَخْزَيْتَهُ وَمَا لِلظَّالِمِينَ مِنْ أَنصَارٍ - 3:192

TIP 290 رَبَّنَا إِنَّنَا سَمِعْنَا مُنَادِيًا يُنَادِي لِلْإِيمَانِ أَنْ آمِنُوا بِرَبِّكُمْ فَآمَنَّا - 3:193

TIP 291 رَبَّنَا فَاغْفِرْ لَنَا ذُنُوبَنَا وَكَفِّرْ عَنَّا سَيِّئَاتِنَا وَتَوَفَّنَا مَعَ الْأَبْرَارِ - 3:193

TIP 292 رَبَّنَا وَآتِنَا مَا وَعَدتَّنَا عَلَى رُسُلِكَ وَلَا تُخْزِنَا يَوْمَ الْقِيَامَةِ إِنَّكَ لَا تُخْلِفُ الْمِيعَادَ - 3:194

TIP 293 بَّنَا ظَلَمْنَا أَنفُسَنَا وَإِن لَّمْ تَغْفِرْ لَنَا وَتَرْحَمْنَا لَنَكُونَنَّ مِنَ الْخَاسِرِينَ - 7:23

365 TIPS

TO HELP YOU MEMORISE THE QUR'AN
'ONE MOTIVATIONAL TIP FOR EACH DAY OF THE YEAR'

REFERENCES

365 TIPS

TO HELP YOU MEMORISE THE QUR'AN
'ONE MOTIVATIONAL TIP FOR EACH DAY OF THE YEAR'

REFERENCES